Drawing
on the _Go!_
Lots of Things

Barbara Soloff Levy

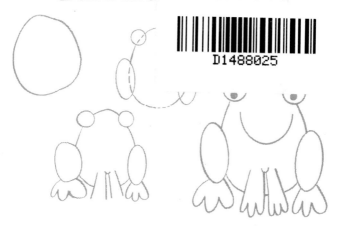

Dover Publications, Inc.
Mineola, New York

Bibliographical Note

Drawing on the Go! Lots of Things, first published by
Dover Publications, Inc., in 2010, is a republication in a different
format of the work originally published as *How to Draw* by Dover
Publications, Inc., in 2001.

International Standard Book Number

ISBN-13: 978-0-486-47945-3
ISBN-10: 0-486-47945-5

Manufactured in the United States by Courier Corporation
47945501
www.doverpublications.com

Note

If you think you can't draw, think again. Follow the easy steps in this little book and you'll be drawing in no time! Using simple shapes, you will find out how to draw a pumpkin, a turtle, a bicycle, a basketball, and much more. Start with the pear on page 2, paying attention to the shapes and lines. You'll be erasing the dotted lines on some pages, so use a pencil. When you have finished your picture, erase the dotted lines and get ready for some more fun—coloring in your pictures any way you wish!

PEAR

Practice Page

APPLE

Practice Page

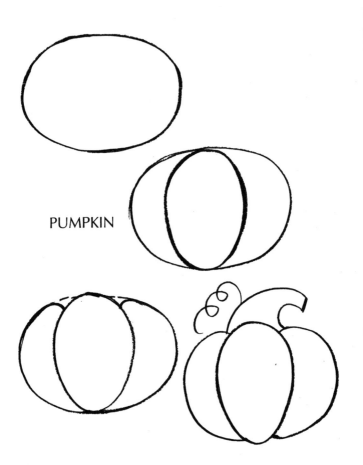

PUMPKIN

Practice Page

PINEAPPLE

8

Practice Page

GRAPES

Practice Page

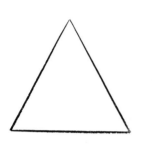

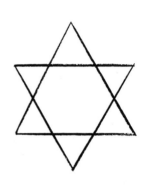

STAR

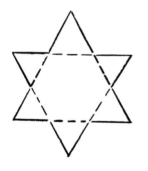

12

Practice Page

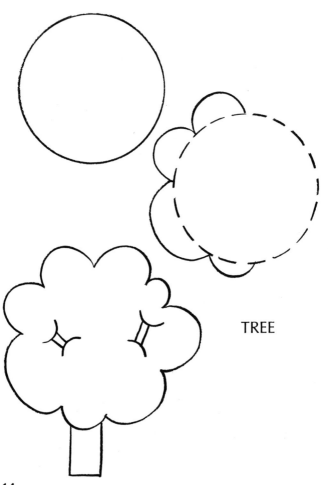

TREE

14

Practice Page

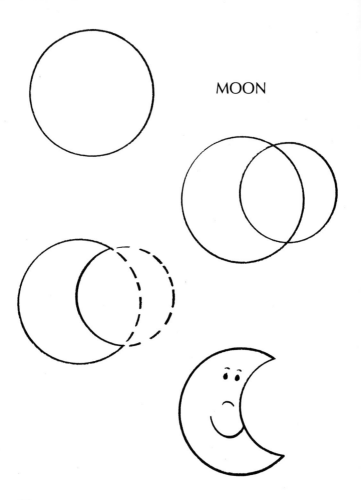

MOON

Practice Page

SUN

Practice Page

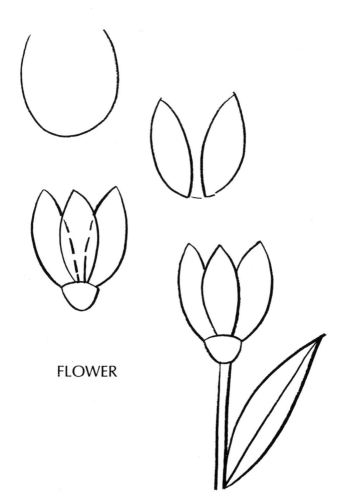

FLOWER

Practice Page

FLOWERPOT
AND FLOWERS

Practice Page

TABLEWARE

Practice Page

DOG

Practice Page

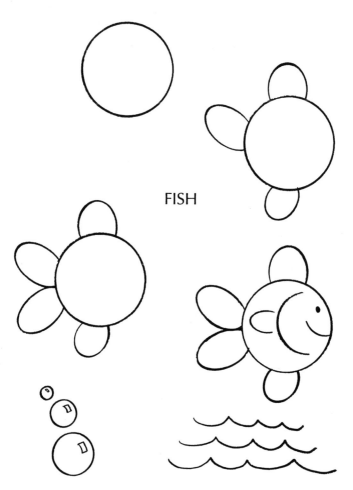

FISH

28

Practice Page

RABBIT

Practice Page

MOUSE

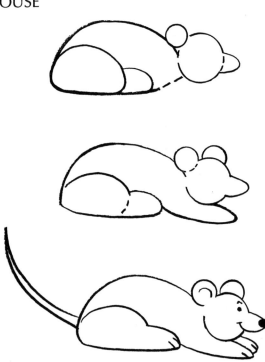

Practice Page

TURTLE

Practice Page

FROG

Practice Page

CAT

Practice Page

BIRD
AND
HOUSE

40

Practice Page

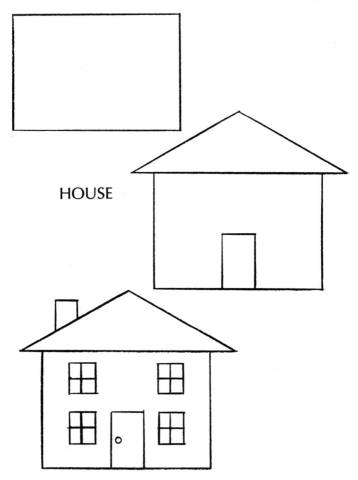

HOUSE

Practice Page

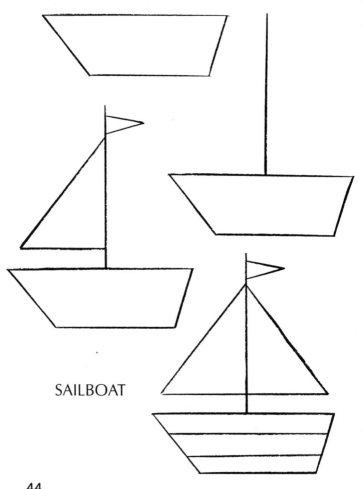

SAILBOAT

Practice Page

CAR

Practice Page

48

Practice Page

COAL CAR

Practice Page

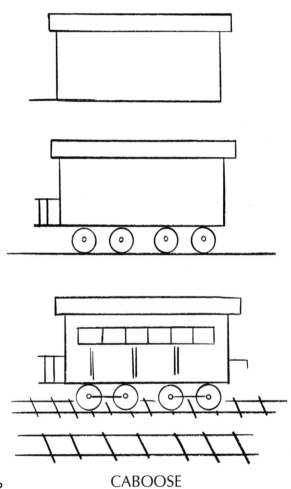

CABOOSE

Practice Page

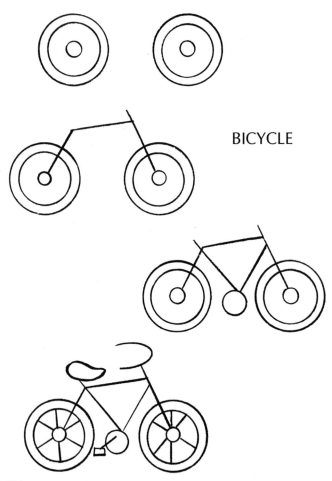

BICYCLE

Practice Page

TRICYCLE

Practice Page

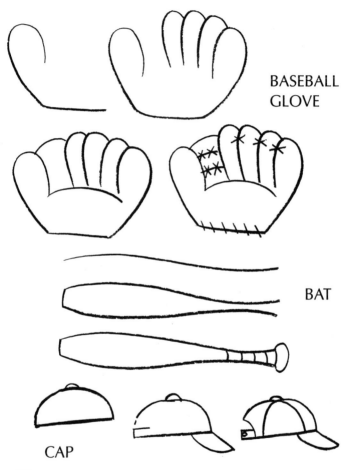

BASEBALL
GLOVE

BAT

CAP

58

Practice Page

BASEBALL

BASKETBALL

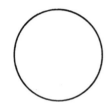 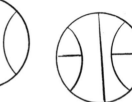

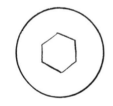  

SOCCER BALL

60

Practice Page